MW00768103

GOD'S ATTRIBUTES

Transformed by His Majesty

SIGNATURE SERIES

NewLife
PUBLICATIONS

God's Attributes: Transformed by His Majesty

Published by
New*Life* Publications
A ministry of Campus Crusade for Christ
375 Highway 74 South, Suite A
Peachtree City, GA 30269

Design and production by Genesis Group

Cover by Koechel Peterson & Associates, Inc., Minneapolis, MN

Printed in the United States of America

ISBN 1-56399-207-8

Unless otherwise indicated, Scripture quotations are from the *New International Version*, © 1973, 1984 by the International Bible Society. Published by Zondervan Bible Publishers, Grand Rapids, Michigan.

Scripture quotations designated NLT are from the *New Living Translation*, © 1996 by Tyndale House Charitable Trust.

CONTENTS

This book, part of the Bill Bright *Signature Series*, is a condensation of *GOD: Discover His Character*, which was published in 1999.

As Members of
Global Founding Partners

the following families are helping to fulfill the Great Commission through helping to train Millions of Pastors around the world.

Bill and Christie Heavener and Family
Ed and Edye Haddock and Family
Stuart and Debbie Sue Irby and Family

FOREWORD

FOR CLOSE TO thirty-five years, Bill Bright has been my mentor and friend. From the first day I met him, he has ministered to me through his contagious enthusiasm for Jesus Christ and the Great Commission. My own walk with Christ is richer, deeper, and more intimate because of what I have learned and observed from Bill. I count it one of the greatest privileges of my life to be mentored by this godly man.

Though he would deny this because of his humility, Bill rightfully deserves a place in history as one of the great spiritual leaders of the Christian faith. Millions of people have placed their faith in Jesus Christ because this one man chose to live a life of total devotion to God. For more than five decades, Bill's influence on our world has left an eternal mark for Christ. His legacy will no doubt continue for generations to come.

When we reach the latter stages of life, it is a natural desire for us to want to build a legacy. We

long to leave something of value to the world
after our own short lives on earth have ended. We
want to believe our lives meant something and we
want to know that we had lasting significance.

Many would build a legacy to serve their own
egos, leaving a name for themselves. But, this cannot be said about Bill. His goal from his first hours
of receiving Christ has been to live his life to glorify God. Bill's legacy stems from his devotion to
his first love—Jesus Christ. This is why I believe
God has blessed him and used him. He has kept
his passion burning for Christ. The abundant evidence found in his life and ministry bears this out
—the deep, intimate walk with God he has en-
joyed for many years, his fifty-plus years of marriage to his beloved wife, Vonette, and a worldwide ministry that has proclaimed the gospel to
millions and touches people in almost every cor-
ner of the world. Bill would be the first person to
say he does not deserve any of the credit. God deserves all the praise and glory for what has happened in his life and ministry.

I have always known Bill to liberally share
with others what God is teaching him. I benefit
greatly from listening to his insights, as countless
others do as well. This is why I am thrilled that he

chose to write *GOD: Discover His Character*, a compilation of his personal, lifelong study of the attributes of God. No one qualifies to write this kind of book, as Bill himself admits. The subject matter is far too grand and enormous. The fullness of God cannot be contained in any one book.

Then again, Bill is the perfect choice to write a book such as this one. If we want to discover the character of God, doesn't it make sense for us to listen to someone who has known Him, walked with Him, served Him, loved Him, and made Him known to millions? With nearly sixty years of his life dedicated to knowing God and making Him known, Bill fulfills those qualifications. He knows what he's talking about. He knows the difference that studying the attributes of God can make in a person's life.

Reading *God's Attributes*, the distilled essence of *GOD: Discover His Character*, is not a dry, academic study, but rather an experience in worship of the living God. Page after page reflects who God is and how He has revealed His character to us in the person of Jesus Christ and in His Word. Bill gives us a glimpse of the greatness of God, the sheer wonder of His majesty, the enormity of His power, and the depth of His love.

Read this book and you can expect two things to happen. First, you will worship and praise God in new and exciting ways. As you reflect on the attributes of God, you cannot help but fall to your knees and worship Him.

Second, your life will change. Is it possible for a Christian, filled with the Spirit, to study the attributes of God without a change in heart and character? No, it's not. When we study God's character, our hearts are stirred to become more like Jesus Christ.

There is a tremendous need for Christians to reflect a Christlike character to our hurting world. Theodore Roosevelt once said, "Character, in the long run, is the decisive factor in the life of an individual and of nations alike." The truth of this statement still resonates with us today. For individuals to change, for nations to change, for the world to change, character is the "decisive factor." And the only person who can change hearts is God. Thankfully, Bill Bright has written this book to point us to God so that studying, reflecting, and delighting in His attributes will, indeed, change our lives.

STEVE DOUGLASS

"WHO ARE YOU, GOD?"

CONSIDER ONE OF the deepest questions in the universe: Is it possible for a mere human, less than a tiny speck on a pebble of a planet in the midst of a vast galaxy, to know the great God who created everything? If so, can we know God well enough to trust Him with the most sensitive areas of our lives?

In our natural condition, it is impossible for us to know God. In fact, if you look around, you will notice that the world barely acknowledges that God exists. Many people are even hostile toward Him.

Our insensitivity to God reminds me of a story. One day a preschooler was riding his tricycle on the sidewalk when his attention was captured by a line of ants scurrying across the driveway. He stopped his trike, got off, and knelt down to peer at the busy insects. After some time, he had a terrible thought. His daddy would be coming home soon and would park right on top of the ant line!

The ants were in danger!

The little boy decided he had to do something, so he shouted at the ants, but they paid no attention. Then he grabbed a big leaf and tried to herd them in another direction, but they just scurried around the leaf and re-formed their doomed line. He didn't know what else he could do. After puzzling over the insolvable problem for a time, the boy lost interest and wandered off to play with his toys.

Have you ever wondered what God sees when He looks down on our little planet? There we all are, billions of humans scurrying here and there, so caught up in our personal plans that we rarely look up. And if we do, how will we actually see God as He is?

In an attempt to know God, people have concocted various ideas about Him. Some consider God to be hard to get along with, someone to fear. Others think of Him as a heartless dictator waiting to punish them for doing wrong. Perhaps you see Him as a kindly grandfather who shakes His head over the terrible plight of mankind but does not get involved in personal lives. Do you see Him as loving, gracious, tender, and compassionate? Or as critical, jealous, vindictive, and haughty?

I hear from many Christians who are discouraged in their quest to know God more fully. They claim to have tried to learn what God is like but have come up short. Maybe they failed on a commitment they made to God and feel the communication lines are down between themselves and heaven. Some simply do not know what God is like and have decided they probably will never know more than they do now. Millions of people cry out, *"Who are you, God?"*

Why Is It Important to Know God?

My desire to write about God began many years ago when Dr. James Montgomery Boice of the "Bible Hour" radio program interviewed me. One of the first questions Dr. Boice asked me was, "What is the most important truth to teach any follower of Christ?"

What an incredible question! No one had ever asked me that before, so I was not prepared to answer it. For a brief moment, I was speechless. But then I am convinced that God's Holy Spirit gave me the answer: "The attributes of God."

I have had years to think about that question and my answer. Today I am more convinced than ever that there is nothing more important to teach another believer than who God is, what He is like, and why or how He does what He does. These attributes of God can be referred to as His character, nature, qualities, or personality.

Yet one of the most tragic trends I have noticed in our churches today is the way believers view God. Renowned author A.W. Tozer writes in his book *The Knowledge of the Holy:*

> *The long view of God entertained almost universally among Christians is the cause of a hundred lesser evils everywhere among us. With our loss of the sense of majesty has come the further loss of religious awe and the consciousness of the divine presence . . . It is impossible to keep our moral practices sound and our inward attitudes right while our idea of God is erroneous or inadequate. If we should bring back spiritual power to our lives, we must begin to think of God more nearly as He is.*[1]

Everything about our lives—our attitudes, motives, desires, actions, and even our words—is influenced by our view of God. Whether our problems are financial, moral, or emotional, whether we are tempted by lust, worry, anger, or insecurity, our behavior reflects our beliefs about God.

What we believe to be true about God's character affects our friendships, our work and leisure activities, the types of literature we read, and even the music to which we listen. If the majority of believers do not have the right view of God, how can our society even begin to see Him as He is? Because of the wrong view of God that predominates in all areas of our culture today, our society is in moral turmoil, and we are in danger of losing our moral soul.

Everything about our lives—our attitudes, motives, desires, actions— is influenced by our view of God.

We can trace all of our human problems to our view of God. A false view of God leads to sin and corruption, and many times cruelty and great human tragedy. On the other hand, a proper understanding of God leads to a life of blessing for oneself and many generations to follow.

How we view God will affect the way we live and relate with others. Consider the couple who takes in a foster child because they know God loves that little one; they may live next door to parents who neglect or abuse their child. One person cheats his customers because he thinks "no one will ever know"; another repays a loan despite severe financial hardships, because he has a reverential respect for a God who notes men's actions and expects honesty.

All of our actions are driven by our views of God and how He interacts with us. Nothing in life could be more important than knowing God accurately.

God Wants Us to Know Him

My deep desire has been to tell people everywhere about our majestic and intimate Creator. But as I set out to write about our glorious and mighty God, I found myself in a predicament. He lives in indescribable splendor beyond my wildest imagination. His character is far above the limited scope of my human understanding. Compared to God, I am less than a mite in this universe of more than a billion galaxies.

Have you ever felt like I do about understanding and knowing our great God? How can we as mere human beings fully grasp any facet of our gloriously incomprehensible God? So why would I attempt to undertake such a seemingly impossible task? More important, why should any of us try to understand who God is?

Through our own ability, we cannot advance

in our knowledge of God beyond a few biographical facts. But God in His love and mercy has taken steps to make Himself known to us in many ways. That's why I am so anxious to share with you, through this book, the truths about God: because I know without a doubt that God wants us to *really know* Him. Since God is so far above us in every aspect, the process begins with Him as He reveals Himself to those who hunger and thirst to know Him.

To find the truth about what God is like, we must turn to His holy Word, the Bible. It gives us a picture of almighty God. The Bible tells us that although all facets of God's nature are always present, He reveals Himself in three primary ways:

- *God reveals Himself as our great Creator.* Genesis 1, the first chapter in the Bible, unveils the Creator's mighty works, His unlimited power, and eternal knowledge. Our Creator has no limitations.

- *God reveals Himself as our perfect Judge.* The remainder of the Old Testament shows how God built a nation of people dedicated to Him and how He led and blessed these people. Throughout this historical account, God gives laws and promises that establish His nature as one of holiness and integrity. As our Judge, God is perfectly holy, truthful, righteous, and just.

- *God reveals Himself as our gracious Savior.* In the New Testament, God sent His only Son to earth as Savior of the world. Jesus is the flesh-and-blood image of God with whom we can relate. His life, death, and resurrection prove God's love, mercy, and faithfulness.

Would you not agree that the most astounding news we can ever hear is that God, the almighty Creator of heaven and earth, invites us to have an intimate relationship with Him? I can assure you from my own experience that knowing God intimately can transform your life into one of passion, joy, adventure, and peace.

One important principle about God's nature is that all the attributes of God are interactive and completely interrelated. With our human limitations, we dissect God's nature into parts or attributes so we can understand them, but that is not how they exist in God's character. Each attribute is perfectly complete and fully a part of God's personality. As we explore these attributes, keep in mind that if we exalt one of God's qualities over another, we can get a distorted view of His character. In fact, overemphasizing any one of God's attributes to the exclusion of others can lead to heresy. For example, teaching only about God's mercy and neglecting His role as a judge will prevent people from understanding God's hatred of sin and the future punishment for wrongdoing. Therefore, as we study each quality individually, we must remember that it is only one aspect of God's magnificent nature.

In the following pages, I would like to present God's character through thirteen "because" statements that will give us a small picture of God's incomprehensible magnificence. These statements can help us understand God's nature, be assured of what He has promised to do for us, and show us how to respond to His glorious character. The first "because" statement will focus our hearts on God's magnificent personality. The remaining twelve are divided into three topics: *Our Great Creator* (God's attributes of ability), *Our Perfect Judge* (God's attributes of integrity), and *Our Gracious Savior* (God's attributes of relationship). Each statement includes two action points for you to take in acknowledging that attribute of God: a worship suggestion and a response to God's majesty. As you explore these truths of our glorious God, I urge you to use the action points to deepen your intimacy with Him.

Because God is a personal Spirit, I will seek intimate fellowship with Him.

God Is a Personal Spirit

Some "religious" people consider God a force, an evil spirit, or something encased in wood or stone. As a result, their concept of God is hazy or impersonal. If God were merely an energy force or a composite of the universe, as New Age philosophies teach, knowing Him personally would be impossible. And if God were merely an idol, made by man's hand of wood or precious metal, our efforts to know Him would be futile. How could a human being have a relationship with an inanimate object?

But the Bible reveals God as a personal Spirit (John 4:24); therefore we can know Him personally. This may seem like such a simple concept, but it is the underlying truth on which we base our understanding of God.

Although He does not have a physical body as we do, He possesses all the characteristics of a personality: He thinks, feels, and wills. The Bible gives us numerous proofs that we can know God personally.

- Many Old and New Testament believers knew God and were considered His friends. God called Abraham, the "father" of the Hebrew nation, "My friend" (Isaiah 41:8). Moses met with God "face to face" when he talked with God in the tabernacle. In the New Testament, Jesus told His disciples, "Now you are My friends" (John 15:15).

- God has names. Most couples use great care in giving their newborn baby a name that has significance to their family. In the same way, each of God's many names reveals something important about His character. In the Bible, He is called I AM, Most High, Eternal God, Lord of Hosts, Living God, Heavenly Father, Almighty, and Jehovah, along with many other names.

- God is described throughout the Bible by a personal pronoun. He is not described as an "it," but as "He," a word that denotes a definite gender and personality. An impersonal force is not described this way.

- God acts as a distinct personality. The Bible consistently demonstrates that God is a conscious, self-aware being, someone who thinks and makes decisions. The Bible tells us that God "speaks," "sees," and "hears" (Numbers 23:19; Genesis 16:13; 1 Kings 8:30). God exhibits a range of emotions from righteous anger to holy jealousy to love and grief.

As we learn more about God's personality, we will find many areas that are hard to understand. This is because God is so far above our limited understanding that we cannot grasp the fullness of His nature. The fact that God is three-in-one is one of these difficult concepts, yet this truth is one of the most important aspects of God's relationship with us. Theologians have called God's triune nature the "Trinity." The members of the Trinity are involved with everything together, yet they also have distinct roles. This is hinted at in the first chapter in the Bible. Genesis 1:26 reads, "Let *us* make man in *our* image" (emphasis added). The plural pronouns "us" and "our" mean that more than one person was involved. Who else but God was present at creation? No one. Therefore, the Trinity in its simplest terms means one

God manifested in three persons with three distinct roles.

God the Father is the first person of the Trinity. In general, He orchestrates action. For example, He sent to earth God the Son, Jesus, and bestowed His authority upon Him.

God the Son is the second person of the Trinity. Jesus Christ is fully God and fully human. He is the cornerstone and the head of the worldwide Church. Jesus now sits at the right hand of God the Father and is interceding for His Church.

God the Holy Spirit, the third person of the Trinity, is our Comforter. As the "active arm" of God on earth, He lives within believers and guides us into all truth. He convicts us of sin and helps us know God and His will.

It's important to understand the mysterious relationship between the three members of the Trinity because this truth underlies all the work of God. These are a few examples:

- God the Father orchestrated creation. God the Son performed the work of creation. God the Holy Spirit was also involved (Genesis 1:1; Colossians 1:16; Psalm 104:30).

- All three members agreed on Christ's birth in human form. Christ's baptism, which marked the beginning of His earthly ministry, was attended and approved by all three members (Luke 1:35; Matthew 3:16,17).

- Jesus' resurrection was the work of the Trinity: God the Father raised Christ from the dead. Jesus laid down His life and took it up on His own accord. The Holy Spirit was the power in the resurrection (Acts 2:32; John 10:18; Romans 1:4).

- All three members of the Trinity participate in the miracle of the new birth when a person becomes a child of God (1 Peter 1:2).

- All three members of the Trinity participate in the atonement—when we receive forgiveness of our sins. And then all three persons of the Trinity come to live in the new believer's life (Hebrews 9:14; John 14:15–23).

Each member of the Trinity has His own role to play, but each is fully God. God is not three separate Gods like some might envision, but has complete unity. No person in the Trinity is less important, less powerful, or less of anything than

any other person in the Trinity. That personhood
includes the qualities of being infinite (He has no
limits, boundaries, or end), self-existent (He was
not created but has always existed outside of the
created order), eternal (He has never had a beginning and will have no end), and self-sufficient (He
is not dependent on anyone or anything). These
four basic qualities of God are integral to each of
His other attributes.

Worship

As we discover the character of our heavenly Father, we will want to seek His presence and fellowship. Worship is our response to God that shows our gratitude for
who He is. An important part of worshiping God is praising Him. In a quiet time,
praise God for the unlimited qualities of
His personhood. Meditate on these sec-
tions of Scripture: He is infinite—1 Kings
8:27. He is self-existent—Colossians 1:16,
17; Hebrews 1:3. He is eternal—Psalm
90:1,2; 1 Timothy 1:17. He is self-sufficient—Acts 17:25.

We Can Develop an Intimate Relationship with Him

Today, after more than fifty years of getting to know God, I have more joy in the Lord's presence than I have ever had. My communication with Him grows sweeter and sweeter. There is no one in the universe with whom I would rather spend time than my heavenly Father. I do not have adequate words to describe to you the many things He has done for me and the marvelous ways He has guided my life to make it an exciting adventure. My number one priority in life is to maintain my love for Him and to demonstrate my love by my obedience.

To this end, my wife, Vonette, and I begin every day on our knees reading His holy, inspired Word and surrendering the activities of our day to His guidance. I want to be a suit of clothes for the Lord Jesus. I invite Him to walk around in my body as His temple. My heart's passion is to let Him think with my mind, love with my heart, speak with my lips, and continue to seek and save the lost through me.

As we explore other amazing attributes of our glorious Lord, I encourage you to walk and talk with Him, worship and praise Him, and give Him your cares and worries. As you do, you will discover that He, in all His perfect character, wants to have an intimate relationship with you. He yearns to be your loving Savior and wrap His strong arms around you. You need never feel lonely or abandoned again.

Response

Here is a prayer you might pray as we begin our journey to know God more intimately:

Dear God, I want to know You as You really are, the Creator of the universe, our heavenly Father, who holds everything in Your hand. You know my past, present, and future. Help me to love, trust, and obey You with all of my heart, soul, mind, and will. Thank You for giving me an opportunity to know You intimately as my heavenly Father and to tell others about You and Your marvelous love. Amen.

OUR GREAT CREATOR
(Attributes of Ability)

WHEN I TOUR a historic mansion and scrutinize the building's quality and design, I can draw some conclusions about its builder. Is the foundation strong? Is it well-designed? How carefully are the intricate details constructed?

We live on a grand estate called Earth. As we look at the beauty and intricacies of our residence, we marvel at the genius of its design. When we gaze up into the heavens, we are overcome with awe at the vastness of what our great Creator has brought into being. King David describes how nature testifies to the power of God:

> *The heavens declare the glory of God; the skies proclaim the work of His hands. Day after day they pour forth speech; night after night they display knowledge. There is no speech or language where their voice is not heard. Their voice goes out into all the earth, their words to the ends of the world (Psalm 19:1–4).*

To get just a small idea of God's creative power, consider our universe. We live on one of nine planets that revolve around the sun. As the dominant light of our solar system, our sun gives off far more energy in one second than humankind has produced since creation. With a diameter of approximately 860,000 miles, the sun could hold one million planets the size of Earth. Yet our sun is only an average-size star.

Our sun is just one among 100 billion stars in our Milky Way galaxy. If the Milky Way were compared to the size of the North American continent, our solar system would be about the size of a coffee cup!

One of our neighbors, the Andromeda Spiral galaxy, is 2 million light-years away and contains about 400 billion stars. No one knows how many galaxies there are in the universe, but scientists estimate that there are billions of them.[2]

Yet, with the unfathomable vastness of our universe, God spoke and the heavens and earth came into being; He laid the foundations of the world. As His Word tells us, His invisible qualities—His eternal power and divine nature—can be clearly seen and understood from His creation (Romans 1:20).

Because God is all-powerful, He can help me with anything.

God is Omnipotent

God's trait of being all-powerful is called *omnipotence*. Whatever God chooses will come to pass because He has the omnipotent ability to make it happen. God told Isaiah, "My purpose will stand, and I will do all that I please" (Isaiah 46:10). Speaking to God, Job acknowledged, "I know that You can do all things; no plan of Yours can be thwarted" (Job 42:2). Consider some of the things our almighty God can do without any effort.

God has the power to create anything from nothing. The psalmist writes, "The Lord merely spoke, and the heavens were created. He breathed the word, and all the stars were born . . . Let everyone stand in awe of Him. For when He spoke, the world began! It appeared at His command" (Psalm 33:6–9, NLT).

God has the power to sustain everything He has created. The ongoing existence of all creation depends on our all-powerful God every second of every day. The writer of Hebrews affirms: "The Son . . . sustains the universe by the mighty power of His command" (Hebrews 1:3, NLT).

God also has the power to judge sin and rebellion. While one of the great mysteries of life is why God allows evil on the earth, we can know for sure that God will use His mighty power for the destruction of evil. He has given us numerous examples in His Word, such as the great flood in Noah's time and the judgment of Sodom and Gomorrah. We can rest on the fact that every injustice will be righted; every act of sin and rebellion will be accounted for.

Worship

Using Scripture to praise God is an effective way of showing Him how much you love and revere Him. Meditate on these words from Jeremiah 32:17–19:

Ah, Sovereign LORD, you have made the heavens and the earth by Your great power and outstretched arm. Nothing is too hard for You …O great and powerful God, whose name is the LORD Almighty, great are your purposes and mighty are Your deeds.

God Uses His Power in Our Behalf

If creation has so much purpose and design, then human history must also have purpose and design. In His Word, God shows that He has a plan for this world and every person in it: "I have a plan for the whole earth, for My mighty power reaches throughout the world" (Isaiah 14:26, NLT).

First Corinthians 1:24 tells us that God demonstrates His power through His Son. We can see evidence of this in Jesus' virgin birth. God planned before the foundation of the world to send His Son to die for us.

God's ultimate display of power was raising Jesus Christ from the dead. After Jesus' death by crucifixion, His enemies put a Roman seal on the tomb and set guards to ensure no one disturbed His body. Yet their efforts meant nothing to God. When He was ready to display His power, He simply rolled the stone away from the tomb and Jesus walked out alive and well.

Any power that we have comes ultimately from God, the one who has all power. King David acknowledged in one of his prayers, "In Your hands are strength and power to exalt and give strength to all" (1 Chronicles 29:12). Paul writes that the power available to us as believers is "the same mighty power that raised Christ from the dead and seated Him in the place of honor at God's right hand in the heavenly realms" (Ephesians 1:19,20, NLT). Like Paul, we can honestly say, "I can do everything through Him who gives me strength" (Philippians 4:13).

God is seeking faithful servants to be channels of His incredible power. Let me mention five ways God wants to use us to reflect His glory:

- *God gives us power to conquer evil forces*. His power is infinitely greater than the forces of evil. We can apply that truth to our own battle with Satan and his helpers—no matter what they throw at us.

- *God gives us power to live a holy life*. We can be holy vessels of the all-powerful God by committing to live holy lives and being filled with and controlled by the Holy Spirit.

- *God gives us power in our weakness*. His ways are always above our ways, and when we submit to His will, He gives us peace and builds patience into our lives. God uses our weaknesses to highlight His magnificent power.

- *God gives us power to proclaim the gospel.* One important aspect of living a holy life is spreading the good news of God's love and forgiveness to everyone we meet.

- *God gives us power to fulfill His plan for our lives.* He wants to strengthen us so we can serve Him in the fulfillment of His purposes. That plan includes allowing us to have the privilege of making an eternal difference in the lives of others.

Response

Do you feel incapable of doing something that God wants you to do? Rather than concentrating on your inadequacies, focus on God who "is able to do immeasurably more than all we ask or imagine, according to His power that is at work within us" (Ephesians 3:20). By faith, allow God to work through you to accomplish what He desires.

Because God is ever-present,
He is always with me.

God Is Omnipresent

God is present everywhere at the same time. How does He do it? This is how God explains His presence when speaking to Jeremiah: "Am I only a God nearby, and not a God far away?...Do not I fill heaven and earth?" (Jeremiah 23:23,24).

God's ability to be present everywhere is called *omnipresence*. It means that there is not a sliver of space anywhere in the universe where He is not dynamically and powerfully present with all of His wonderful personal attributes. Everywhere throughout the world, to the utmost reaches of the universe, and in heaven, God is always and immediately present with all of who He is! God is not limited by a body, but is a Spirit who moves wherever He wishes.

Many writers have compared God's Spirit-presence to the wind. No one can box it in or stop it from blowing; it comes and goes as it pleases. No one can see the wind, yet we can see its result. Its massive strength is displayed in roiling tornadoes, hurricanes, and typhoons. The wind can also be gentle, like the whisper of a breeze off the ocean. It can bring the smell of soft rain on the leaves or the freshness of spring through an open window. Is this not like the wonderful contrast of our God who can both topple rulers and calm the fears of a little child?

Solomon, the king who was given unparalleled wisdom from God, built a temple for our majestic God. Awed by the holy task, Solomon asks, "Will God really live on earth? Why, even the highest heavens cannot contain you. How much less this Temple I have built!" (1 Kings 8:27). Truly, a temple of gold could never contain God, since even the heavens cannot hold Him.

Amazingly, God reveals His presence to us, which allows us to have an intimate relationship with Him. Let us consider several ways in which God manifests His presence to us.

God's "illuminating presence" affects every person. John 1:9 tells us that God has given light to everyone. Like turning on a light in a dark room, the light of God's presence opens our eyes to truth (2 Corinthians 4:6).

God's "inspirational presence" is revealed in special places and at special times. God spoke to

Moses on Mount Horeb through a burning bush. Paul saw the Lord in a blinding light on the road to Damascus. God also makes His presence known to ordinary believers. The setting may be a devotional time, church service, or revival. God chooses the time and place to reveal Himself to us in special ways, and when He does, we never forget the joy of being in His inspirational presence.

God's "incarnate presence" is manifested in Jesus Christ. John tells us, "The Word [Jesus] became flesh and made His dwelling among us... No one has ever seen God, but God the One and Only, who is at the Father's side, has made Him known" (John 1:14,18). Our awesome God was willing to restrict Himself to a physical body so He could live among us and teach us about Himself. This is the most tangible way God has revealed His presence to us.

God's "indwelling presence" resides within every believer. When Jesus left this earth to return to His Father's side, He told His disciples, "I will ask the Father, and He will give you another Counselor [the Holy Spirit] to be with you forever—the Spirit of truth...He lives with you and will be in you" (John 14:16,17).

Our confidence is in the ever-present nature of God. We can be sure that He sees us, walks with us, and loves us no matter where we are.

Worship

God wants us to "consciously" live in His presence every day. You may want to make my daily practice your own by inviting the Lord to live His life in and through you throughout each day. I encourage you to begin praising God during all your activities too. Pay special attention to how God is at work in your life and in the world around you; make Him the focus of your day.

God Is Always With Us

God's presence means that we cannot go anyplace where God is not beside us: "If I go up to the heavens, You are there; if I make my bed in the depths, You are there. If I rise on the wings of the dawn, if I settle on the far side of the sea, even there Your hand will guide me, Your right hand will hold me fast" (Psalm 139:8–10).

In fact, God is present in all our circumstances and during every crisis. God walks with us, gives us strength, understands our pain, and knows how to handle our problems. He will help us if only we ask Him and are willing to do things His way and in His time.

One of the most basic crises each of us will face is our own death. For many people, even some Christians, the fear of leaving this world is very real. That's when the comforting words of Psalm 23:4 ring: "Even though I walk through the valley of the shadow of death, I will fear no evil, for You are with me; Your rod and Your staff, they comfort me."

Jesus promises, "Surely I am with you always, to the very end of the age" (Matthew 28:20). This was given as part of the Great Commission—God's command for us to go into the entire world and preach the gospel and disciple those who come to faith in Christ. It is when we are fulfilling the Great Commission that Jesus' promise to be with us becomes most precious.

I take great comfort that Jesus is with each of our ministry's full-time staff and trained volunteers. His Holy Spirit is the One who works within the hearts of all believers so that His work will be accomplished. You can take comfort in knowing that God is present and working during any ministry He gives you to do. Take courage in knowing that, as you share your faith in Jesus Christ with others, God is with you.

God's omnipresence enables us to be in constant communion with Him and to depend on Him in every situation. Living in God's presence means realizing that God is with you and is vitally concerned about every part of your life. As I keep this in mind, I find that throughout the day the Lord Jesus communicates with me through impressions in my mind that spring from meditating on His Word and talking to Him in prayer.

Response

God is here with us right now and forever —because He is our ever-present God. He is our guide for life and for eternity. Submit every area of your life to Him and invite Him to use you more fully in serving others. Ask Him to give you the words to say to tell others about His majesty.

Because God knows everything, I will go to Him with all my questions and concerns.

God Is Omniscient

Most scientists spend their lives trying to understand and solve the mysteries of life and the universe. But, for our all-knowing God, there are no mysteries. He has a clear understanding of everything that baffles humankind.

Theologians call God's unlimited knowledge *omniscience* (all-knowing). What does God's omniscience mean? Because God knows absolutely everything that can ever be known, He has never had to learn anything. He does not need a computer because all knowledge is instantly accessible to Him and He remembers everything at all times. He is never bewildered or confused or perplexed. He never has to figure something out; everything is always absolutely clear to Him. Nothing ever surprises God; He is always completely aware of all events because He sees everything. Nothing ever turns out differently than He expected or planned.

Only God knows everything about Himself. He knows His own essence and infinite perfections. He knows what is unknowable to anyone else (1 Corinthians 2:11). Jesus tells us, "No one knows the Father except the Son and those to whom the Son chooses to reveal Him" (Matthew 11:27). What we know about God is possible only because He has revealed Himself through creation, the Bible, and Jesus Christ.

Only God knows everything about His creation. Some people believe that our vast and orderly universe originated as a result of a massive explosion known as the "Big Bang." But where did the original matter and energy come from? How could life originate from the dead, inorganic matter of the Big Bang? And why do explosions today create only chaos and destruction instead of order and intricate design that is present throughout the universe?

How foolish to believe that this universe created itself. Truth and knowledge about creation can only originate with God.

Only God knows everything that has ever happened or will happen. Not a single event in all eternity has gone unnoticed by God. He declares, "I am God, and there is no one else like Me. Only I can tell you what is going to happen even before it happens" (Isaiah 46:9,10, NLT).

Some people are intimidated by God because He knows the end from the beginning—and everything in between. Statements like Proverbs 15:3 unnerve them: "The Lord is watching everywhere, keeping His eye on both the evil and the good." They know that He sees their sin, and the God who sees what is done in secret will someday reveal such behavior publicly. On the other hand, God's omniscience is comforting to those who confess their sins as they recognize them. They know their sins have been forgiven.

Worship

One way to worship our incomprehensible Creator is by coming before Him in silence and awe. Shut out everything else; turn off the radio, television, or music, and come into His presence. Thank Him for His forgiveness of your past, and praise Him for the peace He provides in the present, and the hope you can have because He knows your future.

We Can Trust God with Everything

Only God knows us perfectly and intimately. He understands our desires, motives, and thoughts.

Nothing about us escapes His notice. In fact, God knows infinitely more about us than we will ever know about ourselves (Psalm 139:1–4).

God not only knows about us, but He will never forget us. God promises through Isaiah:

> *Can a mother forget the baby at her breast and have no compassion on the child she has borne? Though she may forget, I will not forget you! See, I have engraved you on the palms of My hands (Isaiah 49:15,16).*

The reference to the engraving on the palms of God's hands is a prophecy of Christ's death on the cross when the Roman soldiers drove nails through His hands. The nail holes are eternal reminders that Christ submitted to death because of His love for us. No wonder we can have assurance that God will never forget about us!

As our Creator, He custom-designed us for a unique purpose. He also knows everything about your past. And He loves you unconditionally in spite of your past sin. He will forgive you when you sincerely confess it to Him.

You can be confident that God knows everything you face in the present. Whatever your circumstances, whatever your need, God understands and will go through it with you. And of course He also knows the future He wants for you. He understands our capabilities, opportunities, and life mission. We can trust Him with every moment of our future.

Because of His complete knowledge of you, He knows which choices will lead to His best for you. Jeremiah 29:11 says, "'I know the plans I have for you,' declares the LORD, 'plans to prosper you and not to harm you, plans to give you hope and a future.'" Following His plan leads to the best choices for our lives—right now, in the future, and for eternity. He is willing to share His great knowledge with us. We can rely on Him as our Teacher, Counselor, and Guide into all truth.

Response

God knows all about you and loves you unconditionally. I encourage you—yes, I plead with you—to open your heart to Him and determine to walk with Him regardless of the cost. Remind yourself every day of the truth of our all-knowing God. You will never again feel the same way about your daily personal fellowship with our wonderful God.

*Because God is sovereign, I will
joyfully submit to His will.*

God Is Sovereign

There exists a Royal King whose majesty, splendor, and awesomeness are almost indescribable. Compared to Him, no other ruler or reign is even a blip on the screen of eternity. He does not need to have ceremony or to drape Himself in grandeur to appear more regal. Jewels and wealth mean nothing to Him. This divine Ruler is none other than the Sovereign God. His throne is far above the universe in heaven; He rules over all.

David, himself a king, asked, "Who is this King of glory?" Then he answers his own question, "The LORD, strong and mighty, the LORD, invincible in battle...The LORD Almighty—He is the King of glory" (Psalm 24:8–10, NLT). In one of the final chapters of the Bible, John identifies Jesus Christ as "KING OF KINGS AND LORD OF LORDS" (Revelation 19:16).

The throne of an earthly ruler, however grand, cannot compare to the glories of God. If we took away the royal trappings from any human sovereign, he would look just like us. His honor is derived from ceremonies and the homage paid him by others, which can be removed in a moment. He may have the power of an army behind him, but he is a sinful human just like you and me.

God's reign is different. God does not derive His right to rule from anyone or anything. No title was bestowed on Him by another, and there is no higher authority anywhere than His. His reign is so magnificent that we cannot even comprehend any part of it.

God's rule is supreme, paramount, and absolute. He has power to do anything He wants. He is present everywhere so no one can hide from Him or escape His scrutiny. He is all-knowing, so there is nothing about which He is unaware. God reigns so supremely above His creation that we cannot question any of His actions. Whatever God wants to have happen will happen; His will cannot be thwarted. Daniel explains, "He determines the course of world events; He removes kings and sets others on the throne" (2:21).

Worship
Understanding God's sovereignty causes us to focus on Him, not ourselves. We fall at His feet and give Him everything we

are and have. I urge you to recognize God's sovereignty right now by humbling yourself before Him. Totally and irrevocably submit to His lordship of your life. Worship Him by giving Him everything you own. Anything you "lose" by serving Him He will replace with something so much better. He controls the universe; He will undoubtedly enrich your life with peace, joy, fulfillment, satisfaction, and rewards beyond your wildest imagination!

We Can Let God Direct Our Lives

Does God's sovereignty mean we have no say with Him? Of course not! He does not consider us puppets or slaves. He made us as free moral agents with minds, wills, and emotions. He will not force His love and plans upon us against our wills. Within the context of His master plan, God gives us the freedom to choose. This is a difficult concept to grasp. Let me explain with an illustration. While on a flight to Dallas, I was free to get up and walk around on the jetliner. I had complete freedom—within limits. I could not alter the plane's course. The plane was going to Dallas!

Our relationship with God is like that. We are not robots mechanically programmed to follow His decrees. God has set a course for us that has been charted before the beginning of time. God assures us, "My purpose will stand, and I will do all that I please" (Isaiah 46:10). His master plan for history will be accomplished, whether we choose to work with Him or follow our own stubborn way. Although He allows us to choose and suffer the consequences of our choices, He never relinquishes control of the plans to accomplish His purposes.

Response

I urge you to allow God to direct your life by surrendering your decisions, trials, hurts, and pain to Him. Give Him your joys, accomplishments, and treasures. Unlike an earthly king, God will take what you give Him and multiply blessings in your life. We do not give up anything but pride, sin, and temporal possessions; He gives us back eternal life, joy, spiritual riches, and an eternal reign with Him!

three

OUR PERFECT JUDGE
(Attributes of Integrity)

COLUMNIST RAY COHN writes in the *New York Times*, "I don't want to know what the law is, I want to know who the judge is."[3] How important is a judge? If a judge is unfair, the court case is a mock trial. If the judge is honest and fair, he will fulfill his role so that justice is served and complaints are addressed.

Since God is the most powerful judge in the universe, we must know what He is like to understand His role of judge. What kind of court does He hold? What kind of laws does He uphold? Is His justice fair and impartial?

Today most people ignore God's role as judge of humankind. They go on with their sin as if no one will ever call them to account. Yet throughout the Bible, God's justice is repeatedly presented. Look at a few of the times God acted as judge:

- He sent Adam and Eve out of the Garden of Eden because of their sin.

- He destroyed the wicked cities of Sodom and Gomorrah.

- He sent plagues on Egypt for the Pharaoh's mistreatment of God's people.

- He struck down Ananias and Sapphira when they lied to the Holy Spirit.

- He sent disease into the Corinthian church for not honoring the Lord's Supper.

As we study God's role as the Perfect Judge, we will tackle some of the difficult areas and see the purity of God's moral attributes of integrity. We will learn about His holiness, righteousness, and faithfulness and how they affect our lives. And of course, we will also discover the truth about God's justice, the basic characteristic for a good judge. Once we see how God's attributes of integrity work together, we can have confidence that every action He takes as judge is perfect. As we grow in our intimacy with God, we will also learn how we can be free of the fear of His judgment against sin.

Of all God's attributes, nothing compares to the splendor of His holiness.

Because God is holy, I will devote myself to Him in purity, worship, and service.

God Is Holy

Anyone who has been near a wildfire understands its tremendous power. When it roars through an area, everything is changed. Ancient trees turn into cinders. Buildings are reduced to ashes. Nothing can withstand its fury. In its wake, a wildfire also brings new growth and restoration. It destroys the dead, purifies, and transforms the landscape. It is powerful, beautiful, and awesome. Nothing can bring regeneration like a forest fire.

God's holiness has a far greater power. Moses, who glimpsed God's holiness in the burning bush, asked, "Who among the gods is like You, O LORD? Who is like You—majestic in holiness, awesome in glory, working wonders?" (Exodus 15:11).

Of all God's attributes, nothing compares to the splendor of His holiness. That means His character is perfect in every way. He is totally pure. His moral excellence is the absolute standard of integrity and ethical purity for all within His universe. His holiness never diminishes.

I feel totally inadequate to describe this attribute of God. How can I, or any sinful human being, find the right words to explain how pure and high God is in His holiness? When I think of God's holiness, I am convicted by the sinful nature of my own being. We are all like a man wearing a beautiful white suit who was invited to go down into the depths of a coal mine. In the darkness of the mine, he was not aware that his suit was becoming soiled. But when he resurfaced into the dazzling light of the noonday sun, he was fully aware that his suit had become sooty and dirty. The light of God's holiness reveals the darkness of our sin.

God is absolutely pure and righteous and abhors evil. The prophet Habakkuk says of God, "Your eyes are too pure to look on evil; You cannot tolerate wrong" (Habakkuk 1:13). God's holiness demands consequences for sin. We have broken His laws, His standard of holiness, and His holiness demands that He judge sin, not ignore or excuse it.

None of our manmade standards of behavior meet the requirements of our holy God. God's holiness mandates that we keep all of His laws perfectly at all times. The only way we can come into His presence is by having our sins covered by the blood of the Lamb, Jesus Christ. Only through Christ's payment can our holy Judge extend His mercy to us.

True knowledge of God's holiness always elicits a worshipful response from us. Moses fell to his face before the burning bush. Isaiah said, "Woe is me!" We cannot stand in the presence of God without acknowledging His holiness and recognizing our own sin. When we concentrate on God's holiness—His moral perfections and His absolute purity—the only appropriate response is humble adoration.

Worship

Music can help us express our awe for our Lord. I encourage you to select one of the Christian hymns, such as *Holy, Holy, Holy*, to worship and praise God in song. Also worship God for the Lamb, who bridged the separation between God and the repentant sinner. Read through the words of the classic hymn *The Old Rugged Cross*, then exalt God's holy name as one of His children who has glimpsed His holiness and received His merciful salvation.

We Can Live Holy Lives

A false view of holiness causes many Christians to stop short of complete surrender to God. They have a distorted view of holiness because they define it from a secular viewpoint. These misinformed believers decide that they do not want to give up their lifestyles, pleasures, and pride and allow God to renew their minds.

But we know a secret: We can live a holy life if we yield to the Holy Spirit who came to glorify Jesus Christ. Jesus is the only person to ever live a holy life, and now He resides within every believer through His Holy Spirit. His presence and power give us the strength to live a holy life moment by moment.

To be holy is to be separated from sin, set apart for God's special use. God gives us the ability to experience a whole new life based on His holiness and purity. But we must obey His direction and laws. Obedience is a liberating, cleansing freedom from all unwholesomeness as we let the holiness of God be absorbed into every fiber of our being. This means giving Him reverential respect, turning away from every evil, and walking in His light.

Everyone who has been greatly used by God for the cause of Christ has gone through an experience of "dying to self" as described in Galatians 2:20. It is not until we know the reality of "death of self" that we experience the fullness of Christ living out His life in and through us. My Galatians 2:20 experience happened in the spring of 1951 when Vonette and I signed a contract to become slaves of Christ. I daily reaffirm this contract.

Real life—abundant life—begins with dying to self. God wants our minds and hearts to be filled with His holy qualities. As our lives are transformed, we will project the light of His holiness into the darkness of our evil world.

Response

In order to have a healthy relationship with your loving Father, "die to self" by daily surrendering everything you are and own to Him and dealing with the sin in your life. Search your heart for any hidden sin and confess it to your holy God. Commit yourself to turn away from any temptations with which you struggle.

Because God is absolute truth, I will believe what He says and live accordingly.

God Is Absolute Truth

Most Americans believe in absolute truth, right? Wrong! Truth has been a major casualty in our modern culture. In a study by George Barna of Americans between ages 26 and 44, only 20 percent of those surveyed strongly disagreed with the statement: "There is no such thing as absolute truth; different people can define truth in different ways and still be correct."[4] Shockingly, only 27 percent of those who described themselves as born-again Christians strongly disagreed! Fifty-two percent actually agreed at least somewhat with the statement.[5]

The whole idea that truth is relative contradicts God's Word. Second Timothy 3:16 says, "All Scripture is inspired by God and is useful to teach us what is true and to make us realize what is wrong in our lives. It straightens us out and teaches us to do what is right" (NLT).

If you were to describe absolute truth, what would you say? Absolute truth is internally consistent. No matter which way you approach a true statement, it remains unassailably true. Internal consistency is vital to all of God's attributes.

Also, absolute truth is true for all people in all places at all times. If you say, "Adultery is always wrong," you would be stating an absolute truth. Whether you live in Bangkok, Japan, or the U.S., adultery is still wrong. On the other hand, if you say, "Today, the interest rate for home mortgages in America is 6.5 percent," that is only true for that particular time and place. It is not absolute truth.

Perhaps the most important fact about absolute truth is that it has its source in our holy God. No human can think up or discover a new truth. Truth has always existed in God's nature; He is the author of truth. Moses explains, "God is not a man, that He should lie. He is not a human, that He should change His mind. Has He ever spoken and failed to act? Has He ever promised and not carried it through?" (Numbers 23:19, NLT). Whatever God says is right. Whatever He promises will always be fulfilled.

Because God knows the beginning from the end, not one of His statements ever turns out to be misdirection. He does not shade the truth or leave out an essential part. His absolute truth applies to every situation in history.

Not only is God's truth absolute, but it lasts forever! I encourage you to read Psalm 119, the greatest chapter in the Bible, about the endurance and truth of God's Word. Verse 160 says, "All Your words are true; all Your righteous laws are eternal." We can count on it for eternity.

God wants us to know the absolute truth, so He has taken the initiative to show us truth in several ways: in His Word, the Bible; by the life, death, and resurrection of His Son; and through His Holy Spirit.

God's Word helps us to avoid confusion about what is right or wrong. We cannot complain that we do not have an example of how to put God's truth into practice—we have the truth in the flesh, Jesus Christ. And we cannot excuse ourselves from knowing and following God's truth—we have the indwelling Holy Spirit who leads us into all truth.

Worship

Spirit-filled worship leads us to a reverence for God's truth, which in turn leads us to daily obedience. We put our worship into action when we say "yes" to God's truth in each and every decision of our lives. Prayerfully ask God to show you an area in your life where you can stand up for God's absolute truth. Perhaps you can help high school students to understand the importance of God's command to be sexually pure. Or maybe during a Bible study you can explain the importance of being truthful to your spouse. Be sure to back up your teaching with God's Word.

God's Truth Sets Us Free

Every day, we make decisions based on beliefs and values that we assume are true. Too often, we later discover our beliefs were an illusion of truth, projected by our corrupt society. As John explains, "They are from the world and therefore speak from the viewpoint of the world, and the world listens to them" (1 John 4:5). The world system is controlled by Satan, who is the father of lies (John 8:44), and the world's viewpoint is based on wrong values and misguided purposes, not absolute truth. Its ideas fluctuate with the time, the person, and the culture. Eventually, the world's viewpoint enslaves us to sin. Only God can free us from the deceptions and distortions of the world system.

God's liberating truth is our anchor for life. Solomon said, "Truth stands the test of time; lies are soon exposed" (Proverbs 12:19, NLT). God's truth has endured for thousands of years. Man's "truth" has not. And since God's truth lasts for eternity, its power to free us from sin will never diminish.

God's truth frees us to live as God intends. Jesus said to His followers, "If you hold to my teaching, you are really My disciples. Then you will know the truth, and the truth will set you free" (John 8:31,32). There are several ways God's truth sets us free.

- *We are free from death and damnation.* Jesus said, "I give them eternal life, and they shall never perish; no one can snatch them out of My hand" (John 10:28). This is why our eternity with God is so sure.

- *We are free from bondage to sin and guilt.* Paul writes in Romans 6:22, "Now that you have been set free from sin and have become slaves to God, the benefit you reap leads to holiness, and the result is eternal life." In Jesus we can live freely and joyfully.

- *We are set free from self-centeredness.* Jesus said, "If any of you wants to be My follower, you must put aside your selfish ambition, shoulder your cross, and follow Me. If you try to keep your life for yourself, you will lose it. But if you give up your life for Me, you will find true life" (Matthew 16:24,25, NLT). Only Christ can free us to be more others-centered as we allow Him to live His life through us.

- *We are free from bondage to fear* (Romans 8:15). Through His Holy Spirit, God enables us to live in freedom—if only we will trust and obey Him!

God's truth sets us free from a life of mediocrity and insignificance. Nothing the world offers can even come close to what God has planned. We will be significant only to the degree that we are willing to fulfill the plan for which God has created us.

Response

The choice is ours. Every day we must choose whom we will believe, God or Satan. Those who diligently seek truth in the right places will find only God's truth. Base your life on it because His absolute truth will set you free. Is there something in the last few weeks that you have been untruthful about? First John 1:6 says, "If we claim to have fellowship with Him yet walk in the darkness, we lie and do not live by the truth." Confess it to the Lord and tell the truth to the one you misled. Then determine to always speak the truth.

Because God is righteous, I will live by His standards.

God Is Righteous

Our culture understands the importance of being "right" about certain things. For example, an architect of a hundred-story skyscraper takes immense precautions to have its foundation perfectly level. If the footings are off even a fraction of an inch, there are tremendous consequences. The farther up he builds on an unleveled foundation, the more unstable the skyscraper becomes.

Although most people understand the importance of laying the "right" foundation, they have problems understanding the "rightness" of moral laws. For example, most people divide stealing into categories like "borrowing," petty theft, robbery, and embezzlement, and feel that some categories are okay. Moral laws, they believe, can be bent a little without incurring any penalty. But that is contrary to how God sees His righteous Laws.

God is righteous because He is holy. But His holiness and His righteousness are not the same. Holiness is "a condition of purity or freedom from sin."[6] God's righteousness is "the quality or attribute of God by virtue of which He does that which is right or in accordance with His own nature, will, and law."[7]

In other words, holiness describes God's nature; righteousness describes how God acts according to His holiness. God's laws are holy because they come from His nature. God's standards for enforcing His laws are always righteous. Holiness sets the standard. Righteousness is the result of a relationship that fulfills that standard.

Everything that God does is perfectly right in every way. David tells us, "The LORD is righteous in all His ways and loving toward all He has made" (Psalm 145:17). For God, righteousness is not an external standard that He must adhere to; righteousness is part of His very nature. It is impossible for God to do anything wrong. As a judge, He has never made a wrong determination. He has never had to reverse a decision when He learned more facts. No one can question His judgment in all His actions.

Because God is righteous, He wants righteousness to fill His universe (Psalm 97:2). Therefore, God's spiritual laws are every bit as absolute as His physical laws. If we break God's natural laws, we pay the consequences. For example, if you jump off of the Empire State Building in New York City, the law of gravity will guarantee your death. God's spiritual laws are no less binding. As the perfect Judge and Lawgiver, God is also the law enforcer. His laws lay out the responsibilities for which God holds us accountable. They are a yardstick by which God measures our righteousness. When His laws are broken, He must punish anyone who defies His righteous laws.

Since God's standards for morality and virtue are 100 percent perfect and we are imperfect and inadequate, we can only be righteous as a gift from God. Through our faith in Jesus, He "credits" His own righteousness to our account.

Worship

What is our worshipful response to the knowledge that God gives us the righteousness of Jesus? The Bible contains many examples of prayers that we can offer up to God. One such prayer was written by Paul: "Now may the God of peace make you holy in every way, and may your whole spirit and soul and body be kept blameless until that day when our Lord Jesus Christ comes again. God, who calls you, is faithful; He will do this" (1 Thessalonians 5:23,24, NLT). Make this prayer the cry of your heart, and you can be assured that He will answer this prayer.

God Helps Us Live Righteously

We are so fortunate "that the LORD is gracious and righteous; our God is full of compassion" (Psalm 116:5). Otherwise, we would be doomed by our lack of righteousness. Our righteousness does not depend on what we do, but on the One in whom we place our faith.

There was nothing we could do to earn this gift of grace; we accepted it by faith. When we put our faith in Christ, we received a new nature —one of holiness and righteousness. Christ wants us to display His righteousness in our new life. Yet we cannot live righteously without the enabling of the Holy Spirit.

The only way we can live a righteous life is by submitting our will to the Holy Spirit moment by moment and depending on Him to empower us. Jesus instructs us to "seek first His kingdom and His righteousness" (Matthew 6:33), and as a result, we will enjoy the rewards of righteous living. Seeking God first will lead to a new perspective on life. Old, worldly attachments will seem insignificant and the blessings of righteous living will be apparent.

Response

I challenge you to rearrange your priorities, schedule, and finances to put God first and follow His "right" plan for your life. Adjusting your standards may mean making changes in your life that fit God's leading. If God directs you to change careers, take the necessary steps to do what He asks. If you feel the Holy Spirit guiding you to help with the preschoolers in

Sunday school, willingly give up that Sunday morning class that you enjoy. If God leads you to share His good news in other countries and cultures, step out in faith and respond. The rewards for you and those you serve are exciting and fulfilling.

Because God is just, He will always treat me fairly.

God Is Just

People today are becoming less concerned about doing what is right. Instead, they look for ways to cover their tracks, believing they will never get caught. If their transgression is discovered, they assume they will never be convicted. If they are found guilty, they can always appeal. If the appeal is denied, they will likely serve only a fraction of their sentence anyway.

Since our justice system can often be manipulated, many people mistakenly believe they can manipulate God's system of justice. They think that their excuses and alibis fool God. But oh how wrong they are! God told Jeremiah, "I the LORD search the heart and examine the mind, to reward a man according to his conduct, according to what his deeds deserve" (Jeremiah 17:10). You can always count on God being just. He will always act according to what is morally upright and good.

In fact, justice is not an external system to which God tries to adhere. His justice comes out of His inner being and is based on His holiness, truthfulness, and righteousness. Because He has all the facts at His disposal, He cannot be fooled. His decisions are always based on absolute truth. And when God pronounces judgment, He has the power to carry out the punishment.

God's standard is the benchmark by which all human behavior is measured. God "always acts in a way consistent with the requirements of His character as revealed in His law. He rules His creation with honesty. He keeps His word. He renders to all His creatures their due."[8] In addition, God's attributes assure us of justice. If He were not all-knowing, how could He know whether we sinned wittingly or manipulated the facts to serve our purposes? If He were not present everywhere at once, how could He know all the circumstances surrounding the issue before Him? If He were not all-wise, how could He carry out the judgment in a totally just way?

God will judge every wrong act ever committed, every sinful motive, every evil word. The sentence for these crimes is eternity in a place called hell. But there are those who will live in safety with God in heaven. These are the ones who have accepted Christ's payment for their sin when He died on the cross. Our loving Savior, Jesus Christ, paid the sentence pronounced by the Perfect Judge. God sees these "sinners saved by grace" as righteous in His courtroom. Therefore, they will live eternally in the love, peace, and joy of God's presence.

We cannot thumb our noses at God's righteous principles and not expect to experience the just consequences of our actions. A reverential fear of God will help us avoid doing anything to hinder our relationship with Him.

Worship

I urge you to live in reverential fear of God, continually searching God's Word and examining your heart for sins that you need to confess to Him. One of the greatest truths I have discovered is a concept called "Spiritual Breathing," which is similar to physical breathing. As you become aware of sin in your life, "exhale" by confessing it (1 John 1:9). Then "inhale" by appropriating the power of the Holy Spirit, based on God's command to be filled with the Spirit (Ephesians 5:18). God will fill, enable, and equip you because He promised to hear and answer prayers in accordance with His perfect will (1 John 5:14,15). Practice this spiritual principle whenever you are tempted so that you can live according to God's just standards.

God's Justice Works for Our Good

All believers are saved because God delays His justice. At what age did you discover God's love and forgiveness? At 7 or 37 or 70? Whatever age we received God's promise of eternal life was more than enough time for God to have caused His wrath to fall on us. How many evil deeds had we committed before that day? How many people had we hurt? None of us deserve even one day of life because of our sinful, depraved nature, so we must be grateful for a just God who delays punishment. Truly, God's delayed justice is an opportunity for His mercy to be shown to many.

Our just God is not concerned just with punishing disobedience, but also with rewarding behavior. Yet God will reward only those who have accepted Christ's payment for their sins. Christ will evaluate each believer's life to determine rewards for faithful obedience and service or loss for disobedience. Paul explains, "We must all appear before the judgment seat of Christ, that each one may receive what is due him for the things done while in the body, whether good or bad" (2 Corinthians 5:10).

God will reward especially those who faithfully tell the lost about the Savior. God told Daniel, "Those who are wise will shine like the brightness of the heavens, and those who lead many to righteousness, like the stars for ever and ever" (Daniel 12:3).

None of us deserve even one day of life because of our sinful, depraved nature.

Every believer should desire to hear the Lord Jesus say these words: "Well done, good and faithful servant." Scripture assures us, "God is not unjust; He will not forget your work and the love you have shown Him as you have helped His people and continue to help them" (Hebrews 6:10).

Response

Galatians 6:7 says, "Do not be deceived: God cannot be mocked. A man reaps what he sows." Are you sowing seeds of destruction, or seeds of mercy, justice, and goodness? Examine your motivations in the way you deal with difficult people. Which category do they fall into: destruction or mercy? If you want to reap God's favor and blessings, obey His command to extend mercy.

four

OUR GRACIOUS SAVIOR
(Attributes of Relationship)

THE PLAN SEEMED so wonderful at the time. More than 100,000 people would camp out in a pristine glade in upstate New York where everyone would get along and love each other. This meeting was part of a movement—one that its followers believed would change the world. The movement really began in 1967, which some called the "Summer of Love." The slogan expressed noble ideals: love, not hate; peace, not war. One of its cornerstones was "free love." Hippies thought they could ignore God's standards, as well as thousands of years of social rules, and gratify themselves with free sex.

The Woodstock Festival in the summer of 1969 culminated this national "Love-In." Instead of the expected 100,000 hippies descending on a quiet countryside, 1.5 million long-haired young people wearing beads and feathers flooded the area for three days of music.

Was Woodstock really a place of peace and love? No. Peter Townsend of "The Who," a band that played during Woodstock, said, "What was going on off the stage was just beyond comprehension—stretchers and dead bodies, and people throwing up, and people having [drug] trips...I thought the whole of America had gone mad."[9]

Nudity, sex, and drug dealing were going on everywhere. One young man was crushed in his sleeping bag by a backhoe. And when the uncontrollable crowd went on their way, they left behind acres of trash. The "Summer of Love" had turned into a time of disaster and disappointment.

Love is a universal need of all humanity. But tragically, our world understands very little about true love. We must turn to our Mighty Creator and Perfect Judge to understand what love is all about.

In the New Testament, there were three primary words for love: *eros* (sensual love), *phileo* (brotherly love), and *agape* (unconditional love). Our world speaks mainly of *eros* or *phileo* love, but God's love is *agape*, the purest, deepest kind of love. God's love is not just words on a page, but was demonstrated in the deepest kind of sacrifice—Christ's death on the cross. He truly is our Gracious Savior.

Because God is love, He is unconditionally committed to my well-being.

God Is Love

God is the source of all love. Love is the supreme expression of His personhood and flows out of His goodness. It affects all of His other attributes. The Bible does not say, "God is holiness" or "God is power," but it does tell us, "God is love" (1 John 4:8). God's heart overflows with His supernatural and unconditional love for us.

God's love is the only reason we exist. It is the *why* of creation, whereas His power is the *how*. Love flows from Him as a pure river of grace and mercy without detracting in any way from His holiness and righteousness. Love is our doorway to knowing God intimately.

God's love is a gift to all who will receive it by faith. Nothing we do will make God love us any more; nothing we do will make Him love us any less. He loves us because He is gracious—not because of who we are, but because of who He is.

God's plan for our salvation was set in motion in eternity past (Ephesians 1:4,5). There was never a moment when God did not purpose His love to make the ultimate sacrifice for us. He planned to leave heaven's glory, beauty, and peace and take on the body of a man. You and I, who are not even worthy to call His name, are so loved that we were always on His mind.

Nothing we do will take away God's love for us. Paul writes, "I am convinced that nothing can ever separate us from His love. Death can't, and life can't. The angels can't, and the demons can't. Our fears for today, our worries about tomorrow, and even the powers of hell can't keep God's love away. Whether we are high above the sky or in the deepest ocean, nothing in all creation will ever be able to separate us from the love of God that is revealed in Christ Jesus our Lord" (Romans 8:38,39). We never need fear that His blessings are a disguise for other intentions. All God's actions toward us flow out of His pure love for us—even in our difficulties.

When iron ore is dug out of a mountain, it is worth only a few dollars per ton. But when that ore is placed in a Bessemer furnace and put under tremendous heat and pressure, it is changed into a high grade of surgical steel.

God uses adversity in our lives, not to destroy us, but to build our faith and refine us into the people He wants us to be. He cannot use self-centered weaklings. During difficult times, God assures us that He will work for our good. Only He knows the future and how things will turn out.

Because He loves us, God has prepared an incredible future for us. First He gives us an abundant life on earth. This is not a temporary provision, nor is it available only when we feel holy enough to accept it. In addition, God gives us a heavenly future with Christ. This is the hope of the one loved by God!

Worship

We worship our loving God, not as a religious exercise or ritual, but with a sincere response to the love He has already shown for us! Praise Him when you wake up in the morning, thank Him as you work, and tell Him how much you love Him before you go to sleep. Respond to His limitless, ever-present love for you by expressing your heart of love to Him.

God Helps Us Spread His Love

One day when I was preparing a message, my young son Zac suddenly appeared with his stack of books and sat silently beside me. I was deeply moved to think that there were dozens of places in our home where he could have gone to read. I told him, "Zac, I want you to know how much it means to me that you have come to sit with me."

My heart melted to hear my son say, "That's why I'm here, Dad. I just want to be with you."

When we genuinely realize how much God has sacrificed for us, we will not be able to keep the Good News to ourselves.

In the same way, the heart of God longs for fellowship with us. As our intimate relationship with God deepens, we become more like Jesus. As a result, we are able to love others unconditionally as God loves us (John 15:12).

Who does God want us to love? Jesus taught, "Love your enemies and pray for those who persecute you" (Matthew 5:44). That is difficult, if not impossible, without the ministry of the Holy Spirit in our lives. We are also to love our neighbors, those around us that we come into contact during our daily routine. When we genuinely realize how much God has sacrificed for us, we will not be able to keep the Good News to ourselves. God's love *is* the Good News that we share with those who have no idea what it means to be loved by Christ.

You may confess, "I don't have that kind of love to share with anyone." To experience and share God's supernatural love, claim it by faith. When we *by faith* ask for God's unconditional love for an "unlovable" person to flow through us, we will discover a rekindled love that is alive and well. Sometimes you and I must take the first step, by faith in love. A positive response from others may not always be immediate, but keep on loving and reaching out. There is no power on earth stronger than supernatural love.

Response

Begin right now to love by faith. Make a list of everyone you do not like or have a hard time loving and those who have hurt you. Now ask the Holy Spirit to fill you with love for each person and claim by faith Christ's great love for him. Then the next time you meet him, by faith draw upon God's limitless, inexhaustible, over-whelming love for him. Through the enabling of the Holy Spirit, demonstrate your love by your actions.

Because God is merciful, He forgives me of my sins when I sincerely confess them.

God Is Merciful

The shackled prisoner trembled with fear as he stood before the imposing bench of the toughest, fairest judge in the district. Courtroom observers held their breath, waiting for what they were sure was to come. The judge had no choice but to pronounce a death sentence. There were no appeals for the horrendous crime, no stays of execution allowed.

Suddenly, to everyone's shock, the judge said to the prisoner, "You are guilty. Nevertheless, I love you, in spite of yourself. And because of my love for you, I have decided to take your place. I will take your punishment for you. I will die in your place. You are a free man."

After a stunned moment, courtroom guards unlocked the prisoner's handcuffs and leg irons, removed the judge's robes, and snapped the irons on his wrists and ankles. As the judge was led off to death row, the shocked prisoner numbly walked out of the courtroom door to freedom, tears of gratitude streaming down his cheeks.

This is an allegory of God's mercy. God is the judge. Since He is perfectly just, all His actions must serve the universal law of justice. We are like the prisoner. We all deserve the death sentence because we are all guilty of numerous sins: "All have sinned and fall short of the glory of God" (Romans 3:23). In His fairness, God must carry out the just punishment: "The wages of sin is death" (Romans 6:23). He cannot allow us to inhabit His perfect heaven, that place without a spot of uncleanness, a thought of wrongdoing, or a charge of guilt.

In the supreme act of mercy, God displayed divine favor and forbearance to us guilty offenders. He took our punishments upon Himself. That is what Jesus Christ did for us at Calvary. By His sacrifice, all who put their trust in Him are declared "not guilty" and freed!

Jesus Christ's sacrifice on the cross satisfied God's just nature. God, the divine Judge, showed mercy and clemency for us guilty sinners. At the cross, God's attributes of *both* justice and mercy found complete fulfillment.

God's mercy does not end with forgiveness of our sins. He gives us an abundant life that is much more than we deserve or could ever expect. In His mercy, He provides what we need to begin growing in His Spirit. He shows us compassion as we walk with Him day by day.

What astounds me as an imperfect human is that God genuinely feels pity and compassion for us during our trials and difficulties. We can be sure that our merciful God is beside us through every trial we face and every pain we endure, and will help us live for His glory in every situation. As we listen to His Spirit and obey His Word, we become fulfilled, joyful members of His family.

Worship

The Word of God states in Micah 6:8, "He has showed you, O man, what is good. And what does the LORD require of you? To act justly and to love mercy and to walk humbly with your God." Do you love mercy? Are you quick to forgive? Spend some time with your compassionate God and ask Him to mold you into His image to become a lover of mercy.

God Expects Us to Extend Mercy

One day Peter asked Jesus how many times he had to forgive someone. Peter thought that forgiving seven times was pretty good. "No!" Jesus replied, "seventy times seven!" Then Jesus gave an illustration showing how God views our responsibility to forgive.

One day a king was going over his accounts, settling old debts. He saw that one of his servants owed him millions of dollars, so he ordered the servant brought before him. When the servant arrived, the king demanded that he pay every penny. But the amount was beyond the servant's ability to pay. The king therefore ordered the man and his family sold into slavery to pay the debt. The servant fell before the king and pleaded for mercy. The king felt pity and forgave him this tremendous debt.

What did this servant do then? He found a fellow servant who owed him a few thousand dollars and demanded payment. The friend begged for mercy, but the servant would not forgive him and had him thrown into prison.

When the king heard about it, he was angry! He called in the servant and demanded to know why the man had acted so unforgiving toward his friend when he himself had been forgiven so much. Then the king commanded the servant be thrown into prison until he had paid every penny.

God gave His only Son to die in our place. That is mercy beyond comprehension. How, then, can we ever refuse to give mercy to others when we have received so much mercy ourselves? To the degree that we show mercy to the poor, the wretched, and the guilty, we are like God. Since God richly lavishes His mercy on us, we must show mercy to one another. And that means letting go of all those old hurts caused by others.

One of mercy's rewards is the intimacy we enjoy in our human relationships. Another reward is the intimacy we experience with our Lord. Since mercy is of the highest priority to God, when we are merciful, we become instruments of blessing and enjoy close fellowship with Him.

That is what mercy is all about. It isn't sweeping bad things under the rug (like tolerance) and looking only at the good side. Mercy sees the whole picture, maintains right from wrong, and loves with the whole heart.

Response

Are you harboring any resentment against someone? Did someone wrong you and now you are having difficulty forgiving him? Reread the parable of the ungrateful

servant in Matthew 18. God has bounti-
fully bestowed mercy on you. How ungrateful not to forgive someone who has
wronged you! Obey God and go to that
person today; forgive him and experience
the joy of showing mercy.

*Because God is faithful, I will trust
Him to always keep His promises.*

God Is Faithful

Think of how an automobile engine functions.
Pistons, fan belts, water pumps, and thousands of
moving parts all whirl around within a small space,
generating power. If one piece becomes even a
fraction of an inch out of line, the engine mal-
functions. At the same time, oil and coolant circu-
late to keep the engine running smoothly. The
parts all work together harmoniously as part of
the whole engine.

That is the way God's attributes function too.
We can compare God's faithfulness to the oil in
the engine that keeps the internal parts running
smoothly. God's faithfulness means that each attribute in His character is working at full capacity

at all times. When does God's love fail? Never, because He is faithful. When is God less than holy? Never, because His character is pure and He is always faithful to who He is and what He says.

God's faithfulness is at the core of God's nature. He is always faithful to His own character. He never changes any of His attributes to accommodate someone else's wishes. Paul acknowledged that when he wrote, "The one who calls you is faithful and He will do it" (1 Thessalonians 5:24).

God *always* keeps His covenants, or promises —without fail. Paul writes, "No matter how many promises God has made, they are 'Yes' in Christ. And so through Him the 'Amen' [so be it] is spoken by us to the glory of God" (2 Corinthians 1:20). That is why we can completely trust God's Word. God is perfectly capable of standing behind His Word. But we must claim His generous promises!

God's faithfulness ensures that every attribute we have studied so far is available to us. He wants us to reflect His faithfulness on earth. He is the example; we are His ambassadors to the world. Yet even though we understand this fact, in our humanity, we must grow in our Christian experience. That means exercising our faith in Him daily to build our trust in God as the Faithful One. Each time He proves Himself faithful in our life, our trust will become stronger.

Worship

What can you trust God for today that you were unable to trust Him for yesterday? What circumstances do you struggle with that you can begin turning over to Him? Exercising faith is like exercising a muscle. The more you use it, the stronger it becomes. If you have difficulty trusting God, begin with small steps of faith. Then lengthen these steps in the days to come.

God Enables Us to Be Faithful

Unfaithfulness has become a hallmark of contemporary society. Too often, husbands and wives are unfaithful in keeping their marriage vows. Parents are frequently unfaithful in their commitment to the well-being of their children. Children tend to disobey their parents. Employees do not always serve their employers as they should, and some employers take advantage of those who work for them.

God is the only one we can completely trust because He has the integrity and flawless character that enables Him to be absolutely faithful to His Word and commitments. No one else can fulfill all promises as He does.

The faithfulness of God should cause us to love Him more, study His Word, share the message of salvation with others, and pray without ceasing. Such responses draw us ever deeper into our fellowship with the Savior. As we spend more time with Him, our lives begin to reflect more of His faithfulness in the way we love others and in the mercy we extend.

We all experience hard times such as sickness, danger, financial problems, grief, or depression. God does not promise to prevent problems from coming into our lives, but He does promise to go through them with us. Suffering and death are as much a part of living as eating and breathing, and we can rely on God to use these situations to build character and faith in our lives. As I have relied on God's faithfulness and the promises in His Word, He has proved more than able to walk with me through every situation.

God also promises to protect us from temptation (1 Corinthians 10:13). God knows exactly the limits of what we can bear, and He promises that He will not allow us to get into situations where we are overpowered by temptation.

As we serve God, He faithfully gives us gifts. That starts with giving us everything we need for our life of worship and witness. Our faithful God never gives us an assignment for which He has not prepared us and enabled us. Then God leads us into work experiences and training when we are available to Him. God is also faithful to give us less tangible gifts when we experience suffering, such as the pain of a child turning away from the Lord or the death of a loved one. In these life experiences, God gives us the strength, wisdom, and peace to enable us to reflect His faithfulness through the situation.

This is the glorious promise of God to all who follow Him: "He will keep you strong to the end, so that you will be blameless on the day of our Lord Jesus Christ" (1 Corinthians 1:8). He will keep us faithful so we will be with Him in eternity.

Response
In what area of your life is fear of failure beginning to plague you? You can make it through anything—for our faithful God is

there for you even when you do not feel like a hero of the faith. He is working in your life right now, even though you may not see Him at work or feel His presence. Let His past faithfulness fuel your faith. Then you, too, can be a hero of the faith in whatever situation you face.

Because God never changes, my future is secure and eternal.

God Never Changes

The God of the Bible is the only unchanging Supreme Being. He has never altered one bit of His character or His purpose. That is what I love about our wonderful and marvelous God. I have known Him personally since 1944, and today He is just the same in His holiness and love, His grace and mercy as He was when I first turned my life over to Him. When I get up in the morning to pray, His response will not be different from when I pray to Him at bedtime. When I confront a difficult situation, I have calmness of heart because I know His unchanging Holy Spirit is present to guide me. Theologians refer to this consistency and dependability as God's *immutability*.

The Bible presents the God we worship as One who is the same from eternity to eternity. The writer of the Book of Hebrews compares the immutability of God to His unchanging creation: "They will perish, but You remain; they will all wear out like a garment. You will roll them up like a robe; like a garment they will be changed. But You remain the same, and Your years will never end" (Hebrews 1:11,12). He never changes in His essential being, never varies how He reacts to sinful man, to man's repentance, or to man's worship. Sin and unbelief always displease Him; obedience and faith always warm His heart.

God has never had to learn anything—He has always been omniscient. God has never had to develop talents or skills—He has always been able to do everything. He has never needed to mature —He has always been perfect in all His attributes.

God is not moody, like we are. When I come before Him in prayer, I do not worry that He has just heard prayers of someone who really made Him angry and will take His anger out on me. He is not more loving one day because He feels good and more judgmental the next because He wakes up on the wrong side of the bed. God's purposes, motives, thoughts, and actions are forever the same.

The fact that we can depend on God's immutability is tremendously reassuring for us today. We can proclaim God's message of love and forgiveness without fear that God will change the rules the next day. If God's character does not change, then it follows that His Word does not change either. If His purposes do not change, then the instructions He gives us do not change. The principles throughout the Old and New Testaments are the same.

God sees all of eternity at once, the end from the beginning. That is why we need God's perspective on the events of life—He sees it in ways we do not. As a result, He can take corrective action to keep us from wandering off course or hurting ourselves as we march through life's parade of circumstances and events.

What a great God we have! We can trust Him not to turn against us, for His love is unchanging. We can trust Him for life after death, for He is eternal. That is why the writer of Hebrews could say, "Jesus Christ is the same yesterday and today and forever" (Hebrews 13:8).

> ### Worship
>
> I urge you to take time to enjoy the wonder of God's attributes. As you learn more about His greatness, thank Him, glorify Him, and praise Him for all that He means to you. Let the Holy Spirit fill your mind with His comfort and gentleness. The more you worship and meditate on His attributes, the more you will become like Him. Worship Him through giving, serving, praising, singing, and thanksgiving.

We Can Rest in God

A story is told of a shipwrecked sailor who clung to a rock in great danger until the tide went down. Later a friend asked him, "Didn't you shake with fear when you were hanging on the rock?"

He simply replied, "Yes, but the rock didn't."

Life and its uncertainties may shake us, but God—who is the Rock of Ages—does not move. If we cling to Him, His strength sustains us.

The nation of Israel is the clearest example of this truth. The Lord declared to the people of Israel, "Everything I plan will come to pass, for I do whatever I wish...I have said I would do it, and I will" (Isaiah 46:10,11, NLT). From the day God placed Adam and Eve in the Garden of Eden, God's hand has been leading and guiding His people.

And we are part of His plan! We share His purpose. Paul writes, "We are God's workmanship, created in Christ Jesus to do good works, which God prepared in advance for us to do" (Ephesians 2:10). We no longer need to feel as if we are unimportant in the cosmos. As God's people, we are His loved ones whom He has planned from the beginning to bless and to live forever!

Response

Paul writes in Philippians 1:6, "I am sure that God, who began the good work within you, will continue His work until it is finally finished on that day when Christ Jesus comes back again" (NLT). Because God never changes, He will never change His mind, go back on His word, or leave unfinished what He has started. Every day He is molding you, maturing you, and preparing you to spend eternity with Him —and He will complete what He has begun. What promise can you claim for an area of your life where you know God is helping you change? Use your Bible concordance to find a promise and claim it for your situation.

five

CULTIVATING A HEALTHY FEAR OF GOD

I GREW UP ON my parents' ranch in Oklahoma where my father had a reputation of being one of the best ranchers in the county. Nobody could ride horses like he could. He taught my four brothers and me how to ride wild broncos. Although I learned how to feel comfortable and secure around those big horses, my father raised me to always have a healthy respect for them. I knew that if I was not careful around those powerful wild horses from Montana, I could easily be hurt or even killed if I did something foolish.

As boys growing up on a ranch, we often swam in the lakes and rivers in our county. Once, when I was about 6 or 7 years old, I ventured out into a lake far away from my brothers and friends. Suddenly, my energy gave out and I started to sink. As I went down for the third time, my older brother and one of his friends pulled me out of the water and helped me get my breath. I could have easily drowned that afternoon. Since then, I have had a respect for swimming alone in deep water.

When I was a teenager, my father and uncle taught me how to drive an automobile. I remember the thrill I experienced as I sat behind that steering wheel, stepped on the accelerator, and felt the surge of power thrust me down the country road. Once again, my parents instilled in me a healthy respect, this time for the automobile. I could have been injured or even killed if I acted foolishly behind the steering wheel of that car.

We naturally fear and respect things that have great power or that can alter our lives in the fraction of a second. We treat these things much differently than we do the ordinary objects or people in our lives.

What about God? He is the sovereign Creator and Ruler of our universe. We have glimpsed His power, holiness, and justice. How much respect should we have for Him?

In His Word, God commands us to fear Him. When the Lord was giving the children of Israel the Ten Commandments, He spoke to them from the heart of the fire on Mount Sinai. The people were greatly frightened because they understood they were in the presence of their awesome Creator God. He commanded them to fear Him (Exodus 19:17,18; 20:18–20).

This is only one of many places throughout the Bible where God's people are instructed to fear God. But what does fearing God really mean?

What Does It Mean to Fear God?

God is not some hateful warlord who desires to do us harm. He is not reckless or foolish in the use of His great power, so we will never become random victims of His lack of control. He is not a spooky, hideous creature who hides in the dark to scare us when we least expect it. These are some of the reasons we normally fear someone. But that is not the kind of fear God is talking about. The psalmist records, "The LORD delights in those who fear Him, who put their hope in His unfailing love" (Psalm 147:11). When the Scriptures tell us to fear God, it means we are to have awe, reverence, and respect for our magnificent God.

The following explanation, from *Hard Sayings of the Bible*, helps us understand the phrase "fear the Lord":

> *The term for* fear *can describe everything from dread, or being terrified, to standing in awe or having reverence. When used of the Lord,*

it applies to both aspects of the term, a shrinking back in recognition of the difference or holiness of God and the drawing close in awe and worship. It is an attitude of both reluctance and adoration that results in a willingness to do what God says. The fear of the Lord, then, is absolutely necessary if we are even to begin on the right foot in learning, living, or worshiping.[10]

The relationship between little children and their parents may help us grasp this kind of fear. As a child, I had a loving relationship with my parents and was very close to them. Yet I was very aware that my parents were much bigger and stronger than I was. I knew that if I contradicted their rules I was powerless against them, because my parents had great authority over me. They could give or take away privileges. They expected me to behave within predefined boundaries or face the consequences.

God wants us to approach Him in the same way—with an attitude of humility, submissiveness, and a sense of respect. I believe this is one of the reasons God calls Himself our heavenly Father and us His children. We all cringe when we see children sassing their parents or ignoring their requests. It is against the order of things to see children act that way. How can we behave that way toward God? We must treat Him with the greatest respect as our ultimate authority and guide.

God's Word states, "The fear of the LORD is the beginning of wisdom, and knowledge of the Holy One is understanding" (Proverbs 9:10).

Do You Have a Healthy Fear of God?

Years ago, many Christians were known as God-fearing people. What has happened to our Christian culture for us to lose that distinction?

Over time we developed a distorted view of who God is and lost our sense of reverence, respect, and fear of Him. Instead of seeing God as our sovereign Ruler, He is more commonly viewed as our "buddy" or "pal." Instead of recognizing Him as our awesome Creator and holy Judge, we relegate Him to the position of a peer. We have become too casual with God, even in our places of worship. In the past we referred to such places as holy sanctuaries, houses of prayer, or altars, where the glory of God came down upon His people. Today, we have lost even the sense of the presence of the holy, awesome God among us when we come together to praise, worship, and learn about Him.

Fearing God arises out of a conscious commitment to give God the honor He deserves. This attitude must be cultivated in our daily lives. To do so, ask yourself the following questions:

"Do I have a reverential awe of God?" Certainly, your heart soars when you gaze up at the massive ceiling of a cathedral, at the stars on a clear night, or when you stand at the foot of a snowcapped mountain. How much more should we be overcome by a sense of wonder when considering God who created over 100 billion galaxies by merely speaking them into existence!

Let the thought of our magnificent Creator move you to worship Him in the magnitude of who He is and how far He surpasses anything we could ever begin to imagine with our puny, finite minds. Make it a practice to take time out of each day to meditate on God's glory and to praise Him. Use your favorite worship music or commune with God in the beauty of nature. Look through the Life Applications in this book to find verses that can help you praise and worship God. Or note the Scripture passages that mean a lot to you as you read your Bible, then meditate on them later.

"Do I desire to please God more than people?" If you do not, then you lower God to a human level.

The world values appearance, wealth, and position. God values a heart that is right with Him. To whose voice are you listening? If what others think is more important to you than what God thinks, what does that say about the authority and importance He has in your life?

To give God preeminence in your life, spend more time with Him. That may be as simple as talking to Him during your daily routine. Thank Him for the small blessings He gives you. For each decision, big or small, ask Him what He would have you do. Desire to please Him even in the small details of your life. As you do, your intimacy with God will grow and you will allow God to have first place in your life.

"Do I have a hatred for sin and evil?" God detests sin. The Bible says, "Don't be impressed with your own wisdom. Instead, fear the Lord and turn your back on evil. Then you will gain renewed health and vitality" (Proverbs 3:7,8).

What is your attitude about wickedness, sin, and evil? Do you find yourself tolerating it? Do you view it as not being so bad—especially the sin you commit?

God expects us to oppose those things that He opposes. A good rule to follow is to love what God loves and hate what God hates. Evaluate your life to see what you might be harboring that God detests. Perhaps it is a superior attitude toward people who are different. Or maybe you have a love for something, such as money, a car, or your position, that is greater than your love for God. Each of us has areas that give us trouble. Ask God to help you see the sin in your life for what it is and to help you break the patterns of evil-doing. This is a life-long process. But God will be faithful to deliver you from all sin.

Most of all, spend time in God's Word reading how Joseph, Moses, David, Daniel, Mary, Paul, and others exhibited a healthy fear of God. Remember His promise, "As high as the heavens are above the earth, so great is His love for those who fear Him" (Psalm 103:11).

As we cultivate a healthy fear of God, we will see amazing changes in our lives. God will begin doing things that we never dreamed possible. In our concluding chapter, we will discover how intimacy with God will transform our very lives!

six

OPEN YOUR HEART
TO GOD

WHAT DIFFERENCE are these new insights about God making in your life? God tells us not just to listen to the Word but to follow through and do what it says. Otherwise, we are like the ship's officers on the *Titanic*, who were warned by a nearby ship that icebergs had been sighted, but did nothing with the information. Because they did not act on this knowledge, the great ship struck an iceberg and sank, sending thousands to a watery grave. Truly, knowledge without action is worthless.

We are accountable to God for what we know. We must be careful to fully apply the truth He has given us and allow it to transform our lives. Only then will we experience God's best in our lives and become all God intended us to be.

The truth about God will transform your life. How foolish for any of us to get in the way of God as He lovingly works out His will in our lives. I want to share with you six ways to open up your heart to God and apply to your life the truths you have learned about His majestic character.

1. *Write It on Your Heart*

What we hear and read can easily be forgotten unless we make an effort to remember. Spend time meditating on and memorizing Scripture passages that give insight into who God is and how He desires to be involved with you. Vonette and I regularly meditate on these thirteen statements related to each of the attributes presented in this book:

- Because God is a personal Spirit, I will seek intimate fellowship with Him.

- Because God is all-powerful, He can help me with anything.

- Because God is ever-present, He is always with me.

- Because God knows everything, I will go to Him with all my questions and concerns.

- Because God is sovereign, I will joyfully submit to His will.

- Because God is holy, I will devote myself to Him in purity, worship, and service.

- Because God is absolute truth, I will believe what He says and live accordingly.

- Because God is righteous, I will live by His standards.

- Because God is just, He will always treat me fairly.

- Because God is love, He is unconditionally committed to my well-being.

- Because God is merciful, He forgives me of my sins when I sincerely confess them.

- Because God is faithful, I will trust Him to always keep His promises.

- Because God never changes, my future is secure and eternal.

2. Exalt Your God

As a regular part of your devotional time as well as your Sunday routine, worship God for who He is and for the great things He has done. Praise Him using the many names of God in the Bible and sing praise hymns. Thank God for His magnificent qualities.

3. Trust in God

Whatever your circumstances, keep your eyes on Jesus instead of your problems. The more you grow in your relationship with God, the easier it will be to trust Him with everything.

4. Obey God

If you are a typical Christian, your biggest problem is not that you do not know God's commands, but that, for whatever reason, you selectively obey them. Surrender your will completely and irrevocably to God. Do not allow your prideful, worldly desires to create a rebellious spirit toward God. Humble yourself before Him and depend on the Holy Spirit to help you obey God completely.

5. Reflect His Image

God is certainly concerned with what we do, but He is even more concerned with what we are becoming. He is in the process of making us more and more like His Son. Since we are children of God, our loving Father wants us to act in a way that is consistent with who we are. As members of His royal family, when we serve Him, our actions are consistent with His glorious calling and commission on our lives.

6. Share His Majesty

Are you excited about the new things you have learned about God's magnificent nature? Do His greatness, holiness, and gracious love captivate you? Which truths have been the most life-changing to you? Now ask yourself: How can I possibly keep quiet about my new experiences with God? If someone does not know our wonderful God personally, use your conversation as a springboard to tell him how he can have a relationship with God. As you tell fellow believers what you have learned of God's attributes, they will rejoice with you. You will encourage them in their walk of faith.

What if your life radiated the very nature of God to everyone around you? If you allowed God to live out His love, mercy, faithfulness, and righteousness through you, imagine what a difference it would make in your family, church, neighborhood, and workplace. And what if others in your church were also impacted in this way? Just think how your church could change and what effect this would have on your community and the world!

There is only one word to describe the result: revival. Revival always begins with a renewed view —a correct biblical view—of God. But it starts at the heart of the matter: our sin, disobedience, and pride. It spreads as we hunger for God and begin to worship Him with clean hands and pure hearts. This leads to renewed minds and spiritual eyes to see the awesome character and nature of our great God. The more time you spend with God, the more you will get to know His magnificent attributes and the more you will reflect the radiance of God's presence to those around you.

It is my prayer that these insights into the magnificent character of our awesome God will become the sparks for igniting a revival in your life. Will you invite God to begin a transforming work in you? Commit yourself right now to allowing God to transform you by His majesty!

WOULD YOU LIKE TO KNOW GOD PERSONALLY?

THE FOLLOWING FOUR principles will help you discover how to know God personally and experience the abundant life He promised.

1 *God loves you and created you to know Him personally.*

God's Love
"God so loved the world that He gave His only begotten Son, that whoever believes in Him should not perish, but have eternal life" (John 3:16).

God's Plan
"Now this is eternal life: that they may know you, the only true God, and Jesus Christ, whom you have sent" (John 17:3).

What prevents us from knowing God personally?

2 *Man is sinful and separated from God, so we cannot know Him personally or experience His love.*

Man Is Sinful

"All have sinned and fall short of the glory of God" (Romans 3:23).

Man was created to have fellowship with God; but, because of his own stubborn self-will, he chose to go his own independent way and fellowship with God was broken. This self-will, characterized by an attitude of active rebellion or passive indifference, is an evidence of what the Bible calls sin.

Man Is Separated

"The wages of sin is death" [spiritual separation from God] (Romans 6:23).

This diagram illustrates that God is holy and man is sinful. A great gulf separates the two. The arrows illustrate that man is continually trying to reach God and establish a personal relationship with Him through his own efforts, such as a good life, philosophy, or religion—but he inevitably fails.

The third principle explains the only way to bridge this gulf...

3 *Jesus Christ is God's **only** provision for man's sin. Through Him alone we can know God personally and experience God's love.*

He Died In Our Place

"God demonstrates His own love toward us, in that while we were yet sinners, Christ died for us" (Romans 5:8).

He Rose From the Dead

"Christ died for our sins...He was buried...He was raised on the third day according to the Scriptures ...He appeared to Peter, then to the twelve. After that He appeared to more than five hundred..." (1 Corinthians 15:3–6).

He Is the Only Way to God

"Jesus said to him, 'I am the way, and the truth, and the life; no one comes to the Father, but through Me'" (John 14:6).

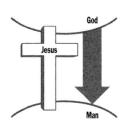

This diagram illustrates that God has bridged the gulf that separates us from Him by sending His Son, Jesus Christ, to die on the cross in our place to pay the penalty for our sins.

It is not enough just to know these three truths...

4 *We must individually **receive** Jesus Christ as Savior and Lord; then we can know God personally and experience His love.*

We Must Receive Christ
"As many as received Him, to them He gave the right to become children of God, even to those who believe in His name" (John 1:12).

We Receive Christ Through Faith
"By grace you have been saved through faith; and that not of yourselves, it is the gift of God; not as a result of works that no one should boast" (Ephesians 2:8,9).

When We Receive Christ, We Experience a New Birth
(Read John 3:1–8.)

We Receive Christ By Personal Invitation
[Christ speaking] "Behold, I stand at the door and knock; if anyone hears My voice and opens the door, I will come in to him" (Revelation 3:20).

Receiving Christ involves turning to God from self (repentance) and trusting Christ to come into our lives to forgive us of our sins and to make us what He wants us to be. Just to agree intellectually that Jesus Christ is the Son of God and that He died on the cross for our sins is not enough. Nor is it enough to have an emotional experience. We receive Jesus Christ by faith, as an act of our will.

These two circles represent two kinds of lives:

Self-Directed Life
S – Self is on the throne
† – Christ is outside the life
● – Interests are directed by self, often resulting in discord and frustration

Christ-Directed Life
† – Christ is in the life and on the throne
S – Self is yielding to Christ
● – Interests are directed by Christ, resulting in harmony with God's plan

Which circle best represents your life?
Which circle would you like to have represent your life?

The following explains how you can receive Christ:

You Can Receive Christ Right Now by Faith Through Prayer
(Prayer is talking with God)
God knows your heart and is not so concerned with your words as He is with the attitude of your heart. The following is a suggested prayer:

> *Lord Jesus, I need You. Thank You for dying on the cross for my sins. I open the door of my life*

and receive You as my Savior and Lord. Thank You for forgiving my sins and giving me eternal life. Take control of the throne of my life. Make me the kind of person You want me to be.

Does this prayer express the desire of your heart?

If it does, I invite you to pray this prayer right now, and Christ will come into your life, as He promised.

How to Know That Christ Is in Your Life

Did you receive Christ into your life? According to His promise in Revelation 3:20, where is Christ right now in relation to you? Christ said that He would come into your life and be your friend so you can know Him personally. Would He mislead you? On what authority do you know that God has answered your prayer? (The trustworthiness of God Himself and His Word.)

The Bible Promises Eternal Life to All Who Receive Christ

"God has given us eternal life, and this life is in His Son. He who has the Son has the life; he who does not have the Son of God does not have the life. These things I have written to you who believe in the name of the Son of God, in order that you may know that you have eternal life" (1 John 5:11–13).

Thank God often that Christ is in your life and that He will never leave you (Hebrews 13:5). You can know on the basis of His promise that Christ lives in you and that you have eternal life from the very moment you invite Him in. He will not deceive you.

An important reminder…

Do Not Depend on Feelings

The promise of God's Word, the Bible—not our feelings—is our authority. The Christian lives by faith (trust) in the trustworthiness of God Himself and His Word. This train diagram illustrates the relationship among *fact* (God and His Word), *faith* (our trust in God and His Word), and *feeling* (the result of our faith and obedience). (Read John 14:21.)

The train will run with or without the caboose. However, it would be useless to attempt to pull the train by the caboose. In the same way, as Christians we do not depend on feelings or emotions, but we place our faith (trust) in the trustworthiness of God and the promises of His Word.

Now That You Have Entered Into a Personal Relationship With Christ

The moment you received Christ by faith, as an act of the will, many things happened, including the following:

- Christ came into your life (Revelation 3:20 and Colossians 1:27).

- Your sins were forgiven (Colossians 1:14).

- You became a child of God (John 1:12).

- You received eternal life (John 5:24).

- You began the great adventure for which God created you (John 10:10; 2 Corinthians 5:17; and 1 Thessalonians 5:18).

Can you think of anything more wonderful that could happen to you than entering into a personal relationship with Christ? Would you like to thank God in prayer right now for what He has done for you? By thanking God, you demonstrate your faith.

To enjoy your new relationship with God...

Suggestions for Christian Growth

Spiritual growth results from trusting Jesus Christ. "The righteous man shall live by faith" (Galatians 3:11). A life of faith will enable you to trust God increasingly with every detail of your life, and to practice the following:

G *Go* to God in prayer daily (John 15:7).

R *Read* God's Word daily (Acts 17:11); begin with the Gospel of John.

O *Obey* God moment by moment (John 14:21).

W *Witness* for Christ by your life and words (Matthew 4:19; John 15:8).

T *Trust* God for every detail of your life (1 Peter 5:7).

H *Holy Spirit*—allow Him to control and empower your daily life and witness (Galatians 5:16,17; Acts 1:8).

RESOURCES

GOD: Discover His Character. Everything about our lives is determined and influenced by our view of God. Through these pages Dr. Bright will equip you with the biblical truths that will energize your walk with God.

GOD: Discover His Character Video Series. In these 13 sessions, Dr. Bright's clear teaching is illustrated by fascinating dramas that bring home the truth of God's attributes in everyday life. This video series, with an accompanying leader's guide, is ideal for youth, college, and adult Sunday school classes or study groups.

First Love: Renewing Your Passion for God. Dr. David Jeremiah stated, "Not until I read Bill Bright's new book, *First Love*, did I understand completely the spiritual dynamic that has driven him for the fifty years of his ministry." Find out how you too can return to a "first love" relationship with the Lord.

Heaven or Hell: The Ultimate Choice. "Where will I go when I die?" The most important question in life only has two possible answers: heaven or hell. And the choice is ours to make. Eternity is a long time to regret a wrong decision. Know the facts about heaven or hell—what God Himself says in the Bible—in this book.

Written by the Hand of God. Although all of Scripture is inspired by God, only the Ten Commandments were truly written by the hand of God. In this practical book, Bill Bright shows how the Old Testament truths about God's standard of holiness are reaffirmed in the New Testament and how the Ten Commandments are relevant to us today.

These and other fine products from *NewLife* Publications are available from your favorite bookseller or by calling (800) 235-7255 (within U.S.) or (407) 826-2145, or by visiting www.nlpdirect.com.

END NOTES

1. A. W. Tozer, *The Knowledge of the Holy* (San Francisco: HarperSanFrancisco, 1961).

2. Pam Beasant, *1000 Facts About Space* (New York: Kingfisher Books, 1992), 10,11.

3. Quoted in Max Boot, *Out of Order* (New York: Basic Books, 1998), 176.

4. *Barna Report, 1997: American Witness* (Dallas: Word Publishing, 1997).

5. George Barna, *What America Believes* (Ventura, CA: Regal Books, 1991), 84-85.

6. Milliard J. Erickson, *Concise Dictionary of Christian Theology* (Grand Rapids, MI: Baker Book House, 1986), 75.

7. Ibid., 144.

8. *Wycliffe Bible Encyclopedia* (Chicago: Moody Press, 1975), 1:981.

9. "1969 Woodstock Festival & Concert" (www.woodstock69.com).

10. Walter C. Kaiser, Jr., et al., *Hard Sayings of the Bible* (Downers Grove, IL: Intervarsity Press, 1996), 284.

William R. Bright

Founder, Chairman, and President Emeritus,
Campus Crusade for Christ International

From a small beginning in 1951, the organization he began now has a presence in 196 countries in areas representing 99.6% of the world's population. Campus Crusade for Christ has more than 70 ministries and major projects, utilizing more than 25,000 full-time and 500,000 trained volunteer staff. Each ministry is designed to help fulfill the Great Commission, Christ's command to help carry the gospel of God's love and forgiveness in Christ to every person on earth.

Born in Coweta, Oklahoma, on October 19, 1921, Bright graduated with honors from Northeastern State University, and completed five years of graduate study at Princeton and Fuller Theological Seminaries. He holds five honorary doctorates from prestigious institutions and has received numerous other recognitions, including the ECPA Gold Medallion Lifetime Achievement Award (2001), the Golden Angel Award as International Churchman of the Year (1982), and the $1.1 million Templeton Prize for Progress in Religion (1996), which he dedicated to promoting fasting and prayer throughout the world.

He has received the first-ever Lifetime Achievement Award from his alma mater (2001).

Bright has authored more than 100 books, booklets, videos and audio tapes, as well as thousands of articles and pamphlets, some of which have been printed in most major languages and distributed by the millions. Among his books are: *Come Help Change the World, The Secret, The Holy Spirit, A Man Without Equal, A Life Without Equal, The Coming Revival, The Transforming Power of Fasting & Prayer, Red Sky in the Morning* (co-author), *GOD: Discover His Character, Living Supernaturally in Christ,* and the booklet *Have You Heard of the Four Spiritual Laws?* (which has an estimated 2.5 billion circulation).

He has also been responsible for many individual initiatives in ministry, particularly in evangelism. For example, the *JESUS* film, which he conceived and financed through Campus Crusade, has, by latest estimates, been viewed by over 4.6 billion people in 236 nations and provinces.

Bright and his wife, Vonette, who assisted him in founding Campus Crusade for Christ, live in Orlando, Florida. Their two sons, Zac and Brad, and their wives, Terry and Katherine, are also in full-time Christian ministry.